My Little Piggies With Wings By

Gloria Guerrero

No Part Of This Publication May Be Reproduced

.

When I was a child on my way home from school I walked through the forest…

…. .

I would find little baby birds on the ground that had fallen out of their nests.

Some had just hatched
from an egg and still

had pieces of egg shell on them.

I would stop to look and the other kids would tell me to leave them, and that there was no more I could do for them.

I paid no attention to what they said.

I took every single baby bird home with me that had a heart beat, cleaned them, and put them in a shoe box lined with soft material that mom had leftover from sewing.

I had different shoe boxes; one for baby birds that were not moving, one for those that were starting to hop, and another for the ones that were ready for flying lessons.

How happy I felt when my baby birds were learning to fly.

They were so chubby from the special food I prepared for them.

I would stand them on a little stick and gently move it while they flapped their little wings.

First thing every morning when they saw me they would open their beaks - ready for the little dropper filled with food.

Mother would feed them and watch over them until I got home from school.

Everyday, they would HOP, HOP, HOP and FLAP, FLAP, FLAP until they were ready to FLY, FLY, FLY.

They looked like little piggies with wings flying AROUND and AROUND and AROUND.

ZOOM, ZOOM, ZOOM, and away they went.

What a HAPPY,
HAPPY, HAPPY
Day!